D1178935

Cats
in
Poetry

Cats
in
Poetry

The ideal gift
for every cat-lover

TEMPUS

In Loving Memory of Poppy

(1989–2007)

R.I.P.

For Alex and Thea

First published 2007

Tempus Publishing
Cirencester Road, Chalford
Stroud, Gloucestershire, GL6 8PE
www.tempus-publishing.com

Tempus Publishing is an imprint of NPI Media Group

British Library Cataloguing in Publication Data.
A catalogue record for this book is available from the British Library.

ISBN 978 0 7524 4432 1

Typesetting and origination by NPI Media Group
Printed and bound in Great Britain

Contents

The Cat

Come, my beautiful cat, on my smitten heart
Keep the claws on your paw in their place,
And let me plunge into your beautiful eyes,
Mingled with metal and agate.

When my fingers languorously caress
Your head and your lissom spine,
And when my hand becomes intoxicated on the pleasure
Of feeling your electric body.

I have my wife in mind. Her look,
Just like yours, kind creature,
Deep and cold, cuts and slits like a spear,

And, from her toes to her head,
A delicate aura, a dangerous perfume,
Float around her dark body.

Charles Baudelaire (1821–1867)

Translated by Evelyne Jate Belle Isle

To a Cat

Stately, kindly, lordly friend
                    Condescend
Here to sit by me, and turn
Glorious eyes that smile and burn,
Golden eyes, love's lustrous meed,
On the Golden page I read.

All your wondrous wealth of hair
                    Dark and fair,
Silken-shaggy, soft and bright
As the clouds and beams of night,
Pays my reverent hand's caress
Back with friendlier gentleness.

Dogs may fawn on all and some
                    As they come;
You, a friend of loftier mind,
Answer friends alone in kind.
Just your foot upon my hand
Softly bids it understand.

A. C. Swinburne (1837–1909)

Tiger at Play

Whence hast thou then, thou witless Puss,
The magic power to charm us thus?
Is it, that in thy glaring eye,
And rapid movements we descry,
While we at ease, secure from ill,
The chimney corner smugly fill,
A lion darting at his prey?
A tiger at his ruthless play?

Joanna Baillie (1762–1851)

Marigold

She moved through the garden in glory,
because
She had very long claws at the ends of her paws.
Her back was arched, her tail was high,
A green fire glared in her vivid eye;
And all the Toms, though never so bold,
Qualied at the martial Marigold.

Richard Garnett

The Lover

Whose Mistresse feared a Mouse,
declareth that he would become a Cat
if he might have his desire.

If I might alter kind,
What, think you, I would be?
Not Fish, nor Foule, nor Fle, nor Frog,
Nor Squirrel on the Tree;
The Fish, the Hooke, the Foule
The lyméd Twig doth catch,
The Fle, the Finger, and the Frog
The Bustard doth dispatch.

The Squirrel thinking nought,
That feately cracks the nut;
The greedie Goshawke wanting prey,
In dread of Death doth put;
But scorning all these kindes,

I would become a Cat,
To combat with the creeping Mouse,
And scratch the screeking Rat.

I would be present, aye,
And at my Ladie's call,
To gard her from the fearfull Mouse,
In Parlour and in Hall;
In Kitchen, for his Lyfe,
He should not shew his hed;
The Pease in Poke should lie untoucht
When shee were gone to Bed.

The Mouse should stand in Feare,
So should the squeking Rat;
All this would I doe if I were
Converted to a Cat.

Attributed to George Tuberville

Sad Memories

They tell me I am beautiful; they praise my
    silken hair,
My little feet that silently slip on from stair
    to stair:
They praise my pretty, trustful face, and
    innocent grey eye;
Fond hands caress me oftentimes—yet
    would that I might die!

Why was I born to be abhorr'd of man and
    bird and beast?
The bullfinch marks me stealing by, and
    straight his song hath ceased;
The shrewmouse eyes me shudderingly,
    then flees; and, worse than that,

The house-dog he flees after me—why was
  I born a cat?

Men prize the heartless hound who quits dry-
  eyed his native land;
Who wags a mercenary tail, and licks a tyrant
  hand.
The lealtrue cat they prize not, that if e'er
  compell'd to roam,
Still flies, when let out of the bag, precipi-
  tately home.

They call me cruel. Do I know if mouse or
  song-bird feels?
I only know they make me light and salutary
  meals:
And if—as 'tis my nature to—ere I devour I
  tease 'em,
Why should a low-bred gardener's boy pursue
  me with a besom?

Should china fall, or chandeliers, or anything
but stocks—
Nay, stocks when they're in flower-pots—the
cat expects hard knocks;
Should ever anything be missed—milk, coals,
umbrellas, brandy—
The cat's pitched into with a boot or anything
that's handy.

"I remember, I remember," how one night I
"fleeted by,"
And gain'd the blessed tiles, and gazed into
the cold, clear sky.
"I remember, I remember, how my little
lovers came;"
And there, beneath the cresecent moon,
play'd many a little game.

They fought—by good St. Catherine, 'twas a
  fearful sight to see
The caol-black crest, the glowing orbs, of one
  gigantic He.
Like bow by some tall bowman bent at
  Hastings Poictiers,
His huge back curved till none obseverd a
  vestige of his ears.

He stood, an ebon crescent, flouting that
  ivory moon,
Then raised the pibroch of his race, the Song
  without a Tune;
Gleam'd his white teeth, his mammoth tail
  waved darkly to and fro,
As with one complex yell he burst, all claws,
  upon the foe.

It thrills me now that final Miaow—that
    weird, unearthly din:
Lone maidens heard it far away, and leap'd
    aout of their skin;
A pot-boy from his den o'erhead peep'd with
    a scared, wan face;
Then sent a random brickbat down, which
    knock'd me into space.

Nine days I fell—or thereabouts—and, had
    we not nine lives,
I wis I ne'er had seen again thy sausage-
    shop,
St. Ives!
Had I, as some cats have, nine lives, how
    gladly I would lick
The hand, and person generally, of him who
    heaved that brick!

For me they fill the milk-bowl up, and cull
  the choice sardine;
But ah! I nevermore shall be the cat I once
  have been!
The memories of that fatal night they haunt
  me even now;
In dreams I see that rampant He, and temble
  at that Miaow.

C.S. Calverley

The Cameronian Cat

There was a Cameronian cat
Was hunting for a prey,
And in the house she catched a mouse
Upon the Sabbath-day.

The Whig being offended
At such an act profane,
Laid by his book, the cat he took,
And bound her to the chain.

"Thou damned, thou cursed creature!
This deed so dark with thee!
Think'st thou to bring to hell below
My holy wife and me?

"Assure thyself that for the deed
Thou blood for blood shalt pay,
For killing of the Lord's own mouse
Upon the Sabbath-day."
The Presbyter laid by the book,
And earnestly he prayed
That the great sin the cat had done
Might not on him be laid.

And straight to execution
Poor Pussy she was drawn,
And high hanged up upon the tree—
The preacher sang psalm.

And, when the work was ended,
They thought the cat near dead;
She gave a paw, and then a mew,
And stretched out her head.

"Thy name," said he, "shall certainly
A beacon remain,
A terror unto evil ones
For everyone. Amen."

Anonymous

Verses on a Cat

A cat in distress,
Nothing more, nor less;
Good folks, I must faithfully tell ye,
As I am a sinner,
It waits for some dinner,
To stuff out its own little belly.

You would not easily guess
All the modes of distress
Which torture the tenants of earth;
And the various evils,
Which, like so many devils,
Attend the poor souls from their birth.

Some living require,
And others desire
An old fellow out of the way;
And which is best
I leave to be guessed,
For I cannot pretend to say.

One wants society,
Another variety,
Others a tranquil life;
Some want food,
Others, as good,
Only want a life.

But this poor little cat
Only wanted a rat,
To stuff out its own little maw;
And it were so good
Some people had such food,
To make them *hold their jaw!*

Percy Bysshe Shelley

A True Cat

Cats I scorn, who sleek and fat,
Shiver at a Norway Rat;
Rough and hardy, bold and free,
Be the cat that's made for me!
He, whose nervous paws can take
My lady's lapdog by the neck;
With furious hiss attack the hen,
And snatch a chicken from the pen.
If the treacherous swain should prove
Rebellious to my tender love,
My scorn the vengeful paw shall dart,
Shall tear his fur, and pierce his heart.

Chorus

Qu-ow wow, quall, wawl, moon.

Anna Seward (1747–1809)

Lament for Tabby

And art thou fallen, and lowly laid,
The housewife's boast, the cellar's aid,
Great mouser of thy day!
Whose rolling eyes, and aspect dread
Whole whiskered legions oft have feld
In midnight battle fray.
There breathes no kitten of thy line
But would have given his life for thine.

Oh, could I match the peerless strain
That wailed for black Sir Roderic slain,
Or that whose milder tone
O'er Gertrude, fall'n in beauty's prime,
The grace of Pennsylvania's clime,
Raised the sepulchral moan!
Such might burst th' eternal bar,
And reach thy spirit from afar.

But thou, remote from pain and strife,
Now reap'st the meed of virtuous life
In some Elysian grove,
Where endless streams of milk abound,
And soft valerian paints the ground
Thy joyous footsteps rove;
With Tasso's cat by poems named,
And Whittington's, in story famed,
Requies cat in pace.

Anonymous

Lines on a Reasonable Affliction

Helen was just slipped into bed:
Her eye-brows on the toilet lay:
Away the kitten with them fled,
As fees belonging to her prey.

For this misfortune careless Jane,
Assure yourself was loudly rated:
And mada, getting up again,
With her own hand the mouse-trap baited.

On little things, as sages write,
Depends our human joy, or sorrow:
If we don't catch a mouse to-night
Alas! no eye-brows for to-morrow.

Matthew Prior 1664–1721)

To My Cat

(Le Chat Noir)

Half loving-kindliness, and half disdain,
Thou comest to my call serenely suave,
With humming speech and gracious gestures grave,
In salutation courtly and urbane:

Yet must I humble me thy grace to gain—
For wiles may win thee, but no arts enslave,
And nowhere gladly thou abidest save
Where naught disturbs the concord of thy reign.

Sphinx of my quiet hearth! who deignst to dwell
Friend of my toil, companion of mine ease,
Thine is the lore of Ra and Rameses;
That men forget dost thou remember well,
Beholden still in blinking reveries,
With some sea-green gaze inscrutable

Graham R. Tomson (1863–1911)

Epitaph for Bathsheba

To whom none ever said scat,
No worthier cat
Ever sat on a mat
Or caught a rat:
Requies-cat

J. G. Whittier (1807–1892)

The Cat and the Rain

Careful observers may foretell the hour
(By sure prognostics) when to dread a shower;
While rain depends, the pensive cat gives o'er
Her frolics, and pursues her tail no more.

Jonathan Swift (1667–1745)

Loulou and her Cat

I'm nervous too, I hate a cat!
Extremely so, but as for that,
It is not only cat or rat,
Or haunted room, or ghostly chat,
That makes my heart go pit-a-pat.

Good pastry is vended
In Cité Fadette;
Maison Pons can make splendid
Brioche and galette.

M'sieu Pons is so fat, that
He's laid on the shelf;
Madmame had a cat that
Was fat as herself.

Long hair, soft as satin,
A musical purr,
'Gainst the window she'd flatten
Her delicate fur.

I drove Lou to see what
These worthies were at—
In rapture she cried, "What
An exquisite cat!

What whiskers! She's purring
All over. Reagle
Our eyes, Puss, by stirring
Your feathery tail!

"M'sieu Pons, will you sell her?"
"Ma femme est sortie,
Your offer I'll tell her;
But—will she?" says he.

Yet Pons was persuaded
To part with the prize:
(Our bargain was aided,
My Lou, by your eyes).

From his légitime save him,
My spouse I prefer,
For I warrant his gave him
Un mauvais quart d'heure.

I'm giving a pleasant
Grimalkin to Lou,
Ah, Puss, what a present
I'm giving to you.

Frederick Locker

(Untitled)

A Cat
I keep, that plays about my
House,
Grown fat
Wih eating many a minching
Mouse.

Robert Herrick (1591–1674)

Love Song

'O lovely Pussy! O Pussy, my love,
What a beautiful Pussy you are,
You are,
You are!
What a beautiful Pussy you are!'

Edward Lear (1812–1888)

Anathema of Cats

On all the whole nacyon
Of cattes wylde and tame;
God send them sorrow and shame!
That cat especyally
That slew so cruelly
My lytell pretty sparowe.

John Skelton (1460–1529)

The Cat and the Canary

An Idyll

I had a little cat, whose name was Tom,
Great-whiskered, tiger-tailed—I loved my cat,
And oft would watch him, as, with sinuous twists,
He strove, with outstretched tongue and yearning jaws,
To catch his fitful and delusive tail,
Barred as a tiger's, but of lesser length,
Comparatively even, for its tip,
Had been curtailed by man's unmanly trap,
Unfeeling to the feline; and he yawned
And yawned again, but never caught his tail,
In short, 'twas short, and would not reach the mouth.
I had a pet canary—on whose voice
Was as a thousand voices all in one,
And Consonant. I loved my little bird;
One of a hundred, doomed to be sold,
But to my special pleasure dedicate,

As bareley-sugar yellow, honey-voiced—
Its name Jemima, for it was a hen.
Yet would I let her out, and she would sit
Upon a high chair's back, unoccupied
And eye me with a sidelong, shifting glance,
Now on one side, now the other of her beak,
Inquisitive of friendly confidence,
As though she read my thoughts and knew the place
Exactly where her beak would pick them out.
My only wife, for young, for I was too old
To be deluded by the husks of corn.
The best of wives, that never uttered sound
Unpleasing, nor embittered by reproof.
I loved to watch her little gurgling throat
Whence issued infinite volumes of sweet sound,

Poured like a river from a tiny vase,
An everlasting wonder to behold—
A wonder ceaseless why she never choked.
I loved my cat, but more I loved my bird
It came to pass Jemima Tommy killed—
I mean Jemima eaten was by Tom.
But soon I learned to make excuse for Tom,
A kitten only, inexperienced,
And pardoned him as a mortal like myself
And other men who do much playful harm,
Squander their youthful "tips" and wonder why,

In years maturer, ends will never meet;
Who hunt, and catch, and kill poor female birds,
Preferring those that carry golden plumes
Or, not to cavil at a letter, "plums."
And they have reason—to poor Tom denied.
Surely such cats are better than such men,
Deserve a milder judgement, happier fate.
But this was an afterthouoght—I hung the cat.

Cosmo Monkhouse (1840–1901)

Mice Before Milk

Let take a cat and fostre hym wel with milk
And tendre flessch and make his couche of silk,
And lat hym seen a mouse go by the wal,
Anon he weyvith milk and flessch and al,
And every deyntee that is in that hous,
Such appetit he hath to ete a mous.

Geoffrey Chaucer (1343–1400)

Montaigne's Cat

'... as the learned and ingenious Montaigne says like himself freely, When my cat and I entertain each other with mutual apish tricks, as playing with a garter, who knows but that I make my cat more sport than she makes me? Shall I conclude her to be simple, that has her time to begin or refuse to play as freely as I myself have? Nay, who knows but that it is a defect of my not understanding her language (for doubtless cats talk and reason with one another) that we agree no better? And who knows better but that she pities me for being no wiser than to play with her, and laughs and censures my folly for making sport for her, when we two play together?'

Izaak Walton (1593–1683)

The Cattie Sits in the Kiln

Ring Spinning

The cattie sits in the kiln-ring,
Spinning, spinning;
And by cam a little wee mousie,
Rinning, rinning.

"Oh what's that you're spinning my loesome,
Loesome Lady?"
"I'm spinning a sark to my young son,"
Said she, said she.

"Weel mot he brook it, my loesome,
Loesome Lady."
"Gif he dinna brook it weel, he may brook it ill."
Said she, said she.

"I soopit my house, my loesome,
Loesome Lady."
"'Tws a sign ye didna sit amang dirt then,"
Said she, said she.

"I fand twall pennies, my winsome,
Winsome lady."
"'Twas a sign a ye warna sillerless,"
Said she, said she.

"I gaed to the market, my loesome,
Loesome lady."
"'Twas a sign ye didna sit at hame then,"
Said she, said she.

"I coft a sheepie's head, my winsome,
Winsome lady."
"'Twas a sign ye kitchenless,"
Siad she, said she.

"I put it in my pottie to boil, my loesome,
Loesome lady."
"'Twas a sign ye didna eat it raw,"
Said she, said she.

"I put it in my winnock to cool, my winsome,
Winsome lady."

"'Twas a sign ye didna burn your chafts then,"
Said she, said she.

By cam a cattie, and ate it a' up my loesome,
Loesome Lady."
"And sae will I you—worrie, worrie, gnash, gnash,"
Said she, said she.

Anonymous

Last Words to a Dumb Friend

Pet was never mourned as you,
Purrer of the spotless hue,
Plummy tail, and wistful gaze,
While you humoured our queer ways,
Or outshrilled your morning call
Up the stairs and through the hall—
Foot suspended in its fall—
While, expectant, you would stand
Arched, to meet the stroking hand;
Till your way your chose to wend
Yonder, to your tragic end.

Never another pet for me!
Let your place all vacant be;
Better blankness day by day
Than companion torn away.

Better bid his memory fade,
Better blot each mark he made,
Selfishly escape distress
By contrived forgetfulness,
Than preserve his prints to make
Every morn and eve an ache.

From the chair whereon he sat
Sweep his fur, nor wince thereat;
Rake his little pathways out
Mid the bushes roundabout;
Smooth away his talons' mark
From the claw-worn pine-tree bark,
Where he climbed as dusk enbrowned
Waiting us who loitered round.

Strange it is this speechless thing,
Subject to our mastering,
Subject for his life and food
To our gift, and time, and mood;
Timid pensioner of us Powers,
His existence ruled by ours,
Should—by crossing at a breath
Into safe and shielded death,
By the merely taking hence
Of his insignificance—
Loom as largened to the sense,
Shape as part, above man's will,
Of the Imperturbable.

As a prisoner, flight debarred,
    Exercising in a yard,
Still retain I, troubled, shaken,
Mean estate, by him forsaken;
And this home, which scarcely took
    Impress from his little look,
        By his faring to the Dim,
    Grows all eloquent of him.

Housemate, I can think you still
    Bounding to the window-sill,
        Over which I vaguely see
Your small mound beneath the tree,
    Showing in the autumn shade
That you moulder where you played.

Thomas Hardy (1840–1928)

Choosing Their Names

Our old cat has kittens three—
What do you think their names should be?

One is tabby with emerald eyes,
And a tail that's long and slender,
And into a temper she quickly flies
If you ever by chance offend her.
I think we shall call her this—
I think we shall call her that—
Now, don't you think that Pepperpot
Is a nice name for a cat?

One is black with a frill of white,
And her feet are all white fur,
If you stroke her she carries her tail upright
And quickly begins to purr.
I think we shall call her this—
I think we shall call her that—
Now, don't you think that Sootikin
Is a nice name for a cat?

One is a tortoiseshell yellow and black,
With plenty of white about him;
If you tease him, at once he sets up his back,
He's a quarrelsome one, ne'er doubt him.
I think we shall call her this—
I think we shall call her that—
Now, don't you think that Scratchaway
Is a nice name for a cat?

Thomas Hood (1799–1845)

On the Death of a Cat

Who shall tell the lady's grief
When her cat was past relief?
Who shall number the hoot tears
Shed o'er her, belov'd for years?
Who shall say the dark dismay
Which her dying caused that day?

Come, ye Muses, one and all,
Come obedient to my call;
Come and mourn with tuneful breath
Each one for a separate death;
And, while you in numbers sigh,
I will sing her elegy.

Of a noble race she came,
And Grimalkin was her name.
Young and old full many a mouse
Felt the prowess of her house;
Weak and strong full many a rat
Cowered beneath her crushing pat;
And the birds around the place
Shrank from her too close embrace.
But one night, reft of her strength,
She laid down and died at length:
Lay a kitten by her side
In whose life the mother died.
Share her line and lineage,
Guard her kitten's tender age,
And that kitten's name as wide
Shall be known as hers that died.
And whoever passes by
The poor grave where Puss doth lie,
Softly, softly let him tread,
Nor disturb her narrow bed.

Christina Rossetti (1830–1894)

Ode

'Twas on a lofty vase's side
Where China's gayest art had dyed
The azure flowers, that blow;
Demurest of the tabby kind,
The pensive Selima, reclined,
Gazed on the lake below.

Her conscious tail her joy declared;
The fair round face, the snowy beard,
The velevt of her paws,
Her coat, that with the tortoise vies,
Her ears of jet, and emerald eyes,
She saw; and purr'd applause.

Still had she gazed; but 'midst the tide
Two angel forms were seen to glide,
The genii of the stream:
Their scaly armour's Tyrian hue
Through richest purple to view
Betray'd a golden gleam.

The hapless nymph with wonder saw:
A whisker first, and then a claw,
With many an ardent wish,
She stretch'd, in vain, to reach the prize
What female heart can gold despise?
What cat's averse to fish?

Presumptuous maid! with looks intent
Again she stretch'd, again she bent,
Nor knew the gulf between.
(Malignant Fate sat by, and smiled)
The slipp'ry verge her feet beguiled,
She tumbled headlong in.

Eight times emerging from the flood
She mew'd to ev'ry wat'ry God,
Some speedy aid to send.
No Dolphin came, no Nereid stirr'd:
Nor cruel Tom, nor Susan heard.
A fav'rite has no friend!

From hence, ye beauties, undeceived,
Know, one false step is ne'er retrieved,
And be with caution bold.
Not all that tempts your wand'ring eyes
And heedless hearts is lawful prize.
Nor all that glitters, gold.

Thomas Gray (1384–1415)

To a Cat

Cat! Who has pass'd thy grand climateric,
  How many mice and rats hast in thy days
  Destroy'd?—How many tit bits stolen? Gaze
With those bright languid segments green, and prick
Those velvet ears—but pr'ythee do not stick
  Thy latent talons in me—and upraise
  Thy gentle mew—and tell me all thy frays
Of fish and mice, and rats and tener chick.
Nay, look not down, nor lick thy dainty wrists—
  For all the wheezy asthma,—and for all
Thy tail's tip is nick'd off—and though the fists
  Of many a maid have given thee many a maul,
Still is that fur as soft as when the lists
  In youth thou enter'dst on glass bottled wall.

John Keats (1795–1821)

An Appeal to Cats in the Business of Love

Ye cats that at midnight spit love at each other,
Who best feel the pangs of the passionate lover,
I appeal to your scratches and your tattered fur,
If the business to love be no more than to purr.
Old lady Grimalkin with her gooseberry eyes,
Knew something when a kitten, for why she was wise;
You find by experience, the love-fit's soon o'er,
Puss! Puss! lasts not long, but turns to *Cat-whore!*
  Men ride many miles,
  Cats tread many tiles,
 Both hazard their necks in the fray;

Only Cats, when they fall
From a house or a wall,
Keep their feet, mount their tails and away!

Thomas Flatman (1637–1688)

From:

Matthias

Rover, with the good brown head,
Great Atossa, they are dead;
Dead, and neither prose nor rhyme
Tells the praises of their prime.
Thou didst know them old and grey,
Know them in their sad decay.
Thou hast seen Atossa sage
Sit for hours beside thy cage;
Thou wouldst chirp, thou foolish bird,
Flutter, chirp—she never stirr'd!
What were no these toys to her?
Down she sank amid her fur;
Eyed thee with a soul resign'd–
And thou deemedst cats were kind!
—Cruel, but composed and bland,

Dumb, inscrutable and grand,
So Tiberius might have sat
Had Tiberius been a cat.

Matthew Arnold (1822–1888)

The Kitten and Falling Leaves

See the kitten on the wall
Sporting with the leaves that fall,
Withered leaves-one-two-and three—
From the lofty elder tree!

* * * *

—But the kitten, how she starts,
Crouches, stretches, paws, and darts!
First at one, and then its fellow
Just as light and just as yellow;
There are many now—now one—
Now they stop and there are none.
What intenseness of desire
In her upward eye of fire!

With a tiger-leap half way
Now she meets the coming prey,
Lets it go as fast, and then
Has it in her power again:
Now she works with three or four,
Like an Indian conjurer,
Quick as he in feats of art,
Far beyond in joy of heart
Were her antics play'd in the eye
Of a thousand standers-by,
Clapping hands with shout and stare,
What would little Tabby care
For the plaudits of the crowd?
Over happy to be proud,

Over wealthy in the treasure
Of her own exceeding pleasure!
'Tis a pretty baby-treat;
Nor, I deem, for me unmeet;
Here, for neither babe nor me,
Other playmate can I see.
Of the countless living things,
That with the stir of feet and wings
(In the sun, or under shade,
Upon bough or glassy blade),

And with busy revellings,
Chirp and song, and murmurings,
Made this orchard's narrow space,
And this vale, so blithe a place;
Multitudes are swept away,
Never more to breathe the day.
Some are sleeping; some in bands
Traveell'd into distant lands;
Others slunk to moor and wood,
Far from human neighbourhood;
And, among the kinds that keep
With us closer fellowship,
With us openly abide,
All have laid their mirth aside.

Where is he, that giddy sprite,
Blue-cap, with his colours bright,
Who was blest as bird could be,
Feeding in the apple tree;
Made such wanton spoil and rout,
Turning blossoms inside out;
Hung with head towards the ground,
Flutter'd, perch'd, into a round
Bound himself, and then unbound,
Lithest, gaudiest harlequin!

Prettiest tumbler ever seen!
Light of heart, and light of limb,
What is now become of him?
Lambs that went through the mountains went
Frisking, bleating merriment,
When the year was in its prime,
They sober'd by this time.
If you look to vale or hill,
If you listen, all is still,
Save a little neighbouring rill.
That from out the rocky ground
Strikes a solitary sound.
Vainly glitter hill and plain,
And the air is calm in vain;

Vainly Morning spreads the lure
Of a sky serene and pure;
Creature none can she decoy
Into open sign of joy:
Is it that they have a fear
Of the dreary season near?
Or that other pleasures be
Sweeter e'en than gaiety?
Yet, whate'er enjoyments dwell
In the impenetrable cell

Of the silent heart which Nature
Furnishes to every creature;
Whatsoe'er we feel and know
Too sedate for outward show—
Such a light of gladness breaks,
Pretty kitchen! from thy freaks—
Spreads with such a living grace
O'er my little Laura's face;
Yes, the sight so stirs and charms
Thee, baby, laughing in my arms,
That almost I couls repine
That your transports are not mine,
That I do not wholly fare
Even as ye do, thoughtless pair!

And I will have my careless season,
Spite of melancholy reason.
Will walk through life in such a way
That, when time brings on decay,
Now and then I may possess
Hours of perfect gladsomeness.
Pleased by any random toy;
By a kitten's busy joy,
Or an infant's laughing eye
Sharing in the ecstasy;

I would fare lie that or this,
Find my wisdom in my bliss;
Keep the sprightly soul awake,
And have faculties to take,
Even from things by sorrow wrought,
Matter for a jocund thought;
Spite of care, and spite of grief,
To gambol with life's falling leaf.

William Wordsworth (1770–1850)

Tiger Eyes

The head sunk low,
The shoulder blades show.
And her whiskers twitch
On the nose an itch.

She sniffs her prey,
Now watch it lay.
Unaware of its fate,
Unprepared for its date.

And now the leap!
The claws sink deep!
She kills for sport
This gentle sort.

Poor mouse that is no more,
Carcass dropped on kitchen floor.
With paws upon her owner's thighs,
A proud look shone in tiger eyes.

P. J. O'Hara

The Retired Cat

A poet's cat, sedate and grave
As poet could well wish to have,
Was much addicted to inquire
For nooks to which she might retire,
And where, secure as mouse in chink,
She might repose, or sit and think.
I know not where she caught the trick—
   Nature perhaps herself had cast her
In such a mould philosophique,
   Or else she learned it of her master.
Sometimes ascending, debonair,
An apple tree, of lofy pear,
Lodged with convenience in the fork,
She watched the gardener at his work;
Sometimes her ease and solace sought
In an old empty watering pot;

There, wanting nothing save a fan,
To seem some nymph in her sedan
Apparelled in exactest sort,
And ready to be borne to court.
  But love of change, it seems, has place,
Not only in our wiser race;
Cats also feel, as well as we,
That's passion's force, and so did she.
Her climbing, she began to find
Exposed her too much to the wind,
And the old utensil of tin

Was cold and comfortless within:
She therefore wished instead of those
Some place of more serene repose,
Where neither cold might come, nor air
Too rudely wanton with her hair,
And sought it in the likeliest mode
Within her master's snug abode.
  A drawer, it chanced, at bottom lined
With linen of the softest kind,
With such as merchants introduce
From India, for the ladies' use,
A drawer impending o'er the rest,
Half open in the topmost chest,
Of depth enough, and none to spare,
Invited her to slumber there;

Puss with delight beyond expression
Surveyed the scene, and took possession.
Recumbent at her ease, ere long,
And lulled by her own humdrum song,
She left the cares of life behind,
   And slept as she would sleep her last,
When in came, housewifey inclined,
The chambermaid, and shut it fast;
By no malignity impelled,
But all unconscious whom it held.
   Awakened by the stock (cried Puss)
'Was ever cat attended thus?
'The open drawer was left, I see,
'Merely to prove a nest for me,
'For soon as I was well composed,
'Then came the maid, and it was closed.

'How smooth these 'kerchiefs, and how sweet!
'Oh what a delicate retreat!
'I will resign myself to rest
'Till Sol, declining in the west,
'Shall call to supper, when, no doubt
'Susan will come and let me out.'
   The evening came, the sun descended,
And Puss remained still unattended.
The night rolled tardily away,
(With her indeed, 'twas never day),

The sprightly morn her course renewed,
The evening gray again ensued,
And puss came into mind no more
Than if entombed the day before.
With hunger pinched, and pinched for room,
She now presaged approaching doom
Nor slept a single wink or purred,
Conscious of jeopardy incurred.

That night, by chance, the poet watching,
Heard an inexplicable scratching;
His noble heart went pit-a-pat,
And to himself he said—'What's that?'
He drew the curtain at his side,
And forth he peeped, but nothing spied.
Yet, by his ear directed, guessed
Something imprisoned in the chest,

And, doubtful what, with prudent care
Resolved it should continue there.
At length a voice which well he knew,
A long melancholy mew,
Saluting his poetic ears,
Consoled him and dispelled his fears:
He left his bed, he trod the floor,
He 'gan in haste the drawers to explore,
The lowest first, and without stop
The rest in order to the top.

For 'tis a truth well known to most
That whatsoever thing is lost,
We seek it, ere it come to light,
In every cranny but the right.
Forth skipped the cat, not now replete
As erst with airy self-conceit,
Nor in her own fond apprehension
A theme for all the world's attention
But modest, sober, cured of all
Her notions hyperbolical,
And wishing for a place of rest
Anything rather than a chest.
Then stepped the poet into bed,
With this reflection in his head.

Moral

Beware of too sublime a sense
Of your won worth and consequence:
The man who dreams himself so great,
And his importance of such weight,
That all around, in all that's done,

Must move and act for him alone,
Will learn in school of tribulation
The folly of his expectation.

William Cowper (1731–1800)

The Cat and the Lute

Are these the strings that poets say
Have cleared the air, and calmed the sea?
Charmed wolves, and from the mountian crests
Made forests dance with all their beasts?
Could these neglected shreds you see
Inspire a lute of ivory
And make it speak? Oh! think then what
Hath been committed by my cat,
Who, in the silence of this night
Hath gnawed these cords, and ruined them quite,
Leaving such remnants as may be
'Frets'—not for my lute, but me.

Puss I will curse thee; mayest thou dwell
With some dry hermit in a cell
Where rat ne'er peeped, where mouse ne'er fed,
And flies go supperless to bed.
Or may'st thou tumble from some tower,
And fail to land upon all fours,
Taking a fall that may untie
Eight of the nine lives, and let them fly.

What, was there ne'er a rat nor mouse,
Nor lander open? nought in the house
But harmless lute-strings could suffice
Thy paunch, and draw thy glaring eyes?

Know then, thou wretch, that every string
Is a cat-gut, which men do spin
Into a singing thread: think on that,
Thou cannibal, thou monstrous cat!

Thou seest, puss, what evil might betide thee:
But I forbear to hurt or chide thee:
For maybe puss was melancholy
And so to make her blithe and jolly,

Finding these strings, she took a snatch
Of merry music: nay then, wretch,
Thus I revenge me, that as thou
Hast played on them, I've played on you.

Thomas Master (1603–43)

From:

Rejoice in the Lamb

For I will consider my cat Jeoffry.

For he is the servant of the living God, duly and daily
serving him.

For at the first glance of the glory of God in the East
he worships in his way.

For this is done by wreathing his body seven times
round with elegant quickness.

For when he leaps up to catch the musk, which is the
blessing of God upon his prayer.

For he rolls upon prank to work it in.

For having done duty and received blessing he begins
to consider himself.

For this he performs in ten degrees.

For first he looks upon his fore-paws to see if they are
clean.

For secondly he kicks up behind to clear away there.

For thirdly he works it upon stretch with the
  fore-paws extended.

For fourthly he sharpens his paws by wood.

For fifthly he washes himself.

For sixthly he rolls upon wash.

For seventhly he fleas himself, that he may not be
  interrupted upon the beat.

For eighthly he rubs himslef against a post.

For ninthly he looks up for his instructions.

For tenthly he goes in quest of food.

For having consider'd God and himself he will
  consider his neighbour.

For if he meets another cat he will kiss her in
  kindness.

For when he takes his prey he plays with it to give it
  [a] chance.

For one mouse in seven escapes by his dallying.

For when his day's work is done his business more
  properly begins.

For he keeeps the Lord's watch in the night against
  the adversary.

For he counteracts the powers of darkness by his
  electrical skin and glaring eyes.

For in his morning orisons he loves the sun and the

sun loves him.

For he is of the tribe of Tiger.

For the Cherub Cat is a term of the Angel Tiger.

For he has the subtlety and hissing of a serpent, which in goodness he suppresses.

For he will not do destruction, if he is well-fed, neither will he spit without provocation.

For he purrs in thankfulness, when God tells him he's a good Cat.

For he is an instrument for the children to learn benevolence upon.

For every house is incomplete without him & a blessing is lacking in the spirit.

For the Lord commanded Moses concerning the cats the departure of the Children of Israel from Egypt.

For every family had one cat at least in the bag.

For the English cats are the best in Europe.

For he is the cleanest in the use of his fore-paws of any quadrupeds.

For the dexterity of his defence is an instance of the love of God to him exceedingly.

For his the quickest to his mark of any creature.

For he is tenacious of his point.

For he is a mixture of gravity and waggery.

For he knows that God is his Saviour.

For there is nothing sweeter than his peace when at rest.

For there is nothing brisker than his life when in motion.

For he is of the Lord's poor and so indeed is he called by benevolence perpetually—Poor Jeoffry! poor Jeoffry! the rat has bit thy throat.

For I bless the name of the Lord Jesus that Jeoffry is better.

For the devine spirit comes about his body to sustain it in compleat cat.

For his tongue is exceeding pure so that it has in purity what it wants in musick.

For he is docile and can learn certain things.

For he can set up with gravity which is patience upon approbation.

For he can fetch and carry, which is patience in employment.

For he can jump over a stick which is patience upon proof positive.

For he can spraggle upon waggle at the word of command.

For he can jump from an emminence into his master's bosom.

For he can catch the cork and toss it again.

For he is hated by the hypocrite and miser.

For the former is afraid of detection.

For the latter refused the charge.

For he camels his back to bear the first motion of business.

For he is good to think on, if a man would express himself neatly.

For he made a great figure in Egypt for his signal services. For he killed the Icneumon-rat very pernicious by land.

For his ears are so acute that they sting again.

For from this proceeds the passing quickness of his atttention.

For by stroking of him I have found out electricity.

For I perceived God's light about him both wax and fire.

For the Electrical fire is the spiritual substance, which God sends from heaven to sustain the bodies both of man and beast.

For God has blessed him in the variety of his movements.

For, tho he cannot fly, he is an excellent clamberer.

For his motions upon the face of the earth are more than other quadrupeds.

For he can tread to all the measures upon the musick.
For he can swim for life.
For he can creep.

Christopher Smart (1722–1771)

Cat Into Lady

A man possessed a Cat on which he doted.
So fine she was, so soft, so silky-coated—
Her very mew had quality!
He was as mad as mad could be.
So one fine day, by dint of supplications,
And tears, and charms, and conjurations,
He worked upon the Powers above
To turn her woman; and the loon
Took her to wife that very afternoon.
Before, 'twas fondness crazed him: now 'twas love!
Never did peerless beauty fire
Her suitor with more wild desire
Than this unprecedented spouse

Th' eccentric partner of her vows.
They spend their hours in mutual coaxing,
He sees each day less trace of cat,
And lastly, hoaxed beyond all hoaxing,
Deems her sheer woman, through and through:
Till certain mice, who came to gnaw the mat,
Disturbed the couple at their bill-and-coo.
The wife leapt up—but missed her chance;
And soon, their fears allayed by her new guise,
The mice crept back: this time she was in stance.
And took 'em by surprise.
Thenceforth all means were unavailing
T' eradicate her little failing.

The bent we are born with rules us till we die.
It laughs at schooling: by a certian age
The vessel smacks, the stuff has ta'en its ply.
Man strives in vain to disengage
His will from this necessity.
Our nature, so confirmed by use,
Binds us in chains that none may loose:

Whips and scorpions, brands and burns,
Leave it as it was before:
If you drive it through the door,
By the window it returns.

Jean de La Fontaine (1621–1695)

Translated by Edward Marsh

From: Life of Johnson

Hodge

I never shall forget the with which he treated Hodge, his cat; for whom he himself used to go out and buy oysters, lest the servants having that trouble should take a dislike to the poor creature. I am, unluckily, one of those who have an antipathy to a cat, so that I am uneasy when in a room with one; and I own, I frequently suffered a good deal from the presence of the same Hodge. I recollect him one day scambling up Dr. Johnson's breast, apparently with much satisfaction, while my friend, smiling and half-whistling, rubbed down his back, and pulled him by the tail; and when I observed he was a fine cat, saying,

'Why, yes, Sir, but I have had cats whom I liked better than this; and then, as if perceiving Hodge to be out of countenance, adding, 'but he is a very fine cat, a very fine cat indeed.'

James Boswell (1740–1795)

From:

Sonnets

Beware, my friend, of fiends and their grimaces;
Of little angels' wiles yet more beware thee;
Just such an one to kiss her did ensnare me,
But coming, I got wounds and not embraces.
Beware of black old cats, with evil faces;
Yet more, of kittens white and soft be wary;
My sweetheart was just such a little fairy,
And yet she well-nigh scratched my heart to pieces.
Oh child! oh sweet love, dear beyond all measure,
How could those eyes, so bright and clear, deceive me?

That little paw so sore a heart-wound give me?—
My kitten's tender paw, thou soft, small treasure—
Oh! could I to my burning lips but press thee,
My heart the while might bleed to death and bless thee.

Heinrich Heine (1797–1856)

Illustrations

The perfect partner to Cats in Poetry!

Dogs
in
Poetry

Often considered 'part of the family', *Dogs in Poetry* justly honours the important role dogs have in millions of people's lives. A dog's capability for unconditional love and unshakeable loyalty make their nature the perfect subject matter for inspiring poetry.

ISBN 978 07524 4390 4

£9.99